ARUBA CERTIFIED CLEARPASS ASSOCIATE – ACCA (HPE6-A67) EXAM PRACTICE QUESTIONS & DUMPS

EXAM STUDY GUIDE FOR ACCA (HPE6-A67)
Exam Prep UPDATED 2020

Presented By: Quantic Books

About Quantic Books:

Quantic Books is a publishing house based in Princeton, New Jersey, USA. , a platform that is accessible online as well as locally, which gives power to educational content, erudite collection, poetry & many other book genres. We make it easy for writers & authors to get their books designed, published, promoted, and sell professionally on worldwide scale with eBook + Print distribution. Quantic Books is now distributing books worldwide.

Note: Find answers of the questions at the last of the book.

QUESTION 1

In what formats can Visual RF Plan export a Bill of Material (Pick two)?

A. Microsoft Excel

B. CSV database format

C. Microsoft Word

D. HTML

E. MySQL

QUESTION 2

Which of the given is NOT accessible for configuration in the startup wizard?

A. RF Plan

B. Administrator and enable passwords

C. Native VLANs on a per port basis

D. WPA-PSK encryption

E. Radius Server

QUESTION 3

Remote AP in tunnel mode, by default, uses which of the given to encrypt user traffic back to the mobility controller?

A. L2TP over IPSec is used to carry user traffic and control traffic

B. PPTP is used to tunnel user traffic

C. The AP does not encrypt user traffic. The user's link layer encryption is used.

D. Remote AP traffic is unencrypted

E. Certificate based tunnel

QUESTION 4

The Guest Provisioning user account has the capacity to do which of the given?

A. Add a new worker to the internal database

B. Change the "look" and "feel" of the guest provisioning page

C. Change the accessible data fields on the guest provisioning page

D. Add a guest user to the internal database

E. Allot a Role to a guest account

QUESTION 5

Which of the given is correct about configuring a server group?

A. Server rules are used to send information to the organized servers

B. A server group can have more than 1 server

C. If the internal database is used in the server group, then no external servers can be added

D. If multiple servers are allotted to the server group, all but the 1st will be overlooked

E. All the servers in a server group will be used round robin style

QUESTION 6

When adding licenses in the startup wizard license screen a reboot is needed:

A. After each license is installed

B. Before any other configuration can take place

C. Just only if the Policy Enforcement Firewall license is installed

D. Once the last License is added

E. A reboot is not needed until you have finished the configuration wizard

QUESTION 7

Guest access can be provided safely by combining the given elements of an Aruba system: (Pick two)

A. Use preventive firewall policies to limit the guest user's access to internal resources

B. Providing guests their own APs and controllers

C. Dedicated Aps

D. Validate users with the internal captive portal beside the internal database or other server

E. DoS guest users off of the system and make them use wired ports

QUESTION 8

802.11n APs operate in which bands? (Pick two)

A. 900 MHz

B. 2.4 GHz

C. 2.4 MHz

D. 5 GHz

E. 5 MHz

QUESTION 9

In decrypt-tunneled forwarding mode, which of the given is correct?

A. User sets up an IPSEC tunnel with the controller

B. The AP decrypts and then the 802.11 frame is sent in a GRE tunnel to the controller

C. The AP decrypts the 802.11 frame and bridges it on the wire

D. The AP decrypts the 802.11 frame, encrypts it as an Ethernet frame and sends it to the controller

E. Users decrypted traffic is sent down the GRE tunnel

QUESTION 10

WPA and WPA2 can use the given verification procedures: (Pick two)

A. WEP Keys

B. PS

C. 802.1X

D. Captive Portal

E. IPSEC

QUESTION 11

Which of the given core elements of ARM enables intelligent distribution of users across accessible channel capacity?

A. Multi-band scan

B. Spectrum load balancing

C. Rogue AP detection

D. Band steering

E. Coordinated Access to a Single Channel

QUESTION 12

Which one of the given file kinds cannot be imported to Visual RF Plan?

A. Dwg

B. Jpg

C. Tiff

D. Gif

E. Bmp

QUESTION 13

Aruba's suggested greatest option for validating guest users is:

A. Temporary worker account

B. Kerberos

C. Captive Portal

D. Windows logon

E. Email address

QUESTION 14

Aliases are used in firewall policies to:

A. Apply firewall polices to ports in a stateful manner

B. Make firewall rules act like traditional ACLs

C. Ease readability and maintainability for source and destination
   addresses

D. Are a part of roles, not the firewall

E. Are implemented as an action in a rule

QUESTION 15

An Aruba AP 125 is proficient of sustaining which of the given network kinds? (Pick three)

A. 802.11b

B. 802.11n

C. 802.11a

D. 802.11w

E. 802.11p

QUESTION 16

What does SET ORIENTATION option do in the Visual RF Plan edit tool?

A. Set the horizontal plane on each floor

B. Give the option to resize a floor

C. Sets the North/South orientation of the building

D. Sets the proper vertical floor plan alignment

E. Lets the planner to set the directional antenna orientation

QUESTION 17

Which of the given is correct of an Aruba Mobility Controller acting as a layer 3 router? (Pick two):

A. The Mobility Controller is the user's default router.

B. The Mobility Controller acts as a bridge.

C. DHCP can be provided by the network infrastructure or the Mobility Controller.

D. The Mobility Controller supports BGP.

E. OSPF needs to be organized

QUESTION 18

Which of these is NOT a valid license type? (Pick two)

A. RFprotect

B. Application Security

C. Base AOS

D. PEF NG

E. Content Security

QUESTION 19

In a Campus AP deployment, an access point has been provisioned statically with an IP address, subnet mask, default gateway and Controller IP address. Control Plane Security has been restricted. Both the Controller and the Access Point are using 6.3 firmware. If a 3rd party firewall is placed in among the AP and controller, what traffic could need to be let for the AP to boot effectively and broadcast Wireless Networks? (Pick two)

A. DHCP

B. PAPI

C. GRE

D. SNMP

E. NTP

QUESTION 20

Web based captive portal can be validated by the given kinds of databases: (Pick two)

A. Internal

B. PEAP

C. RADIUS

D. Kerberos

E. Tacacs

QUESTION 21

What is the IP address of the controller when using the startup wizard?

A. 192.168.1.1

B. 172.16.0.1

C. 10.1.1.1

D. 172.16.0.254

E. 10.1.10.100

QUESTION 22

When local controller is chosen as the controller's operation mode in the startup wizard, which is not anymore configurable?

A. Licenses

B. WLANs

C. VLANs and IP addressing

D. Controller country code

E. Time zone

QUESTION 23

What is NOT a basic configuration in the startup wizard when configuring a WLAN?

A. SSID

B. VLAN

C. Radio Type

D. Antenna Type

E. Firewall Role

QUESTION 24

Which firewall action is needed in a guest pre-verification role to display the captive portal login screen?

A. SRC-NAT

B. DST-NAT

C. permit all

D. permit CP

E. route

QUESTION 25

When a user is blacklisted, the controller will:

A. Send a message telling the user it has been blacklisted

B. De-verify the user from the network but permit it to keep transmitting data

C. Just only block the user if it hasn't yet connected with an AP

D. Stop the user from associating with any SSID on the controller

E. Block the user from the SSID he was connected to

QUESTION 26

Which of the given statements about management accounts is incorrect?

A. The root account can be used to monitor access points connected to the controller

B. The guest-provisioning account can see the controller's configuration but cannot change it

C. The read-only account cannot erase internal database entries

D. The guest-provisioning account can make changes to the internal AP database

E. The network-operations account cannot access configuration

QUESTION 27

802.1X verification takes place:

A. Prior to granting access to L2 media

B. After the user has an IP address

C. After the user sees the captive portal page

D. Prior to the user associating with the AP

E. Once the IPSEC tunnel is up

QUESTION 28

When configuring a default gateway in the startup wizard it needs to be a part of:

A. A VLAN organized with an IP interface and allotted to a port

B. An IP range that is not allotted to a port or VLAN

C. A VLAN allotted to a port but without an IP interface organized

D. A VLAN not organized on the controller

E. The management Vlan

QUESTION 29

A Remote AP uses which type of secure tunnel to communicate with a controller:

A. NAT-T

B. IPSec

C. PPTP

D. GRE

E. IP-IP

QUESTION 30

What type of verification servers are selectable in the WLAN wizard? (Pick three):

A. RADIUS

B. Kerberos

C. LDAP

D. Internal database

E. Tacacs

QUESTION 31

Which of the given information is gathered by APs for the duration ofscanning periods? (Pick three)

A. MAC addresses of neighboring Aps

B. Security threats in thesurroundings

C. Type of non-802.11 interferencedetected

D. Interfering Users connected to otherAps

E. 4.9 GHz devices

QUESTION 32

Visual RF Plan needs some building information when defining a new building. Which one of the given is NOT a user supplied building specification?

A. Building name

B. Longitude and Latitude

C. Attenuation among floors

D. Desired data rate

E. Number of APs

QUESTION 33

What are the four views accessible in Visual RF Plan (Pick four)?

A. User View

B. Controller View

C. Access Point View

D. Floor Plan View

E. Network, Campus and Building View

QUESTION 34

When a barcode scanner connects to an AP, what is the 1st role that is allotted to it?

A. MAC verification default role

B. 802.1X default role

C. Server derived role

D. Initial role

E. User derived Role

QUESTION 35

Which of the given is NOT one of the four continuous functions of ARM?

A. Monitoring the environment for the present operating and substitute channels

B. Collecting and classifying information obtained for the duration ofbackground scans

C. Computing the greatest channel and power level to operate on

D. Make two indices for each AP, for each channel

E. Determining the greatest controller for APs to terminate

QUESTION 36

In what order does the AP dynamically discover the Master controller?

A. DNS query, ADP Broadcast, ADP Multicast, DHCP option 43

B. DHCP option 43, ADP Multicast, ADP Broadcast, DNS query

C. DHCP option 43, DNS query, ADP Multicast, ADP Broadcast

D. ADP Multicast, ADP Broadcast, DHCP option 43, DNS query

E. DHCP option 43, ADP Broadcast, ADP multicast, DNS Query

QUESTION 37

When configuring a guest WLAN via the WLAN section of the startup wizard, which security option is NOT accessible?

A. WEP encryption

B. Direct access to the internet with no captive portal

C. Captive portal with verification via credentials

D. Captive portal with email registration

E. Captive Portal with no verification or registration

QUESTION 38

Which answer properly orders the given AP boot processes as they happen?

A. AP Transfers OS from controller

B. AP builds GRE tunnel to the controller

C. AP determines IP address of the controller

D. AP Radio is enabled

E. a, c, d, b.

F. c, a, b, d.

G. b, d, a, c.

H. a, b, c, d.

I. c, b, a, d.

QUESTION 39

The AP Wizard lets the choice of APs to be provisioned using which of the given procedures (Pick three):

A. APs in particular AP Group

B. All Aps

C. APs designated as Air Monitors

D. APs meeting specified search criteria

E. APs of a specific type

QUESTION 40

Which of the given is NOT accessible for configuration via startup wizard?

A. Controller name

B. Country Code

C. Loopback IP

D. VLAN IP

E. Firewall Roles

QUESTION 41

Firewall policy must be written from:

A. Minimum specific to maximum specific
B. Maximum specific to minimum specific
C. Maximum significant resources first
D. Order is not significant
E. Policies with the most rules 1st

QUESTION 42

How many roles must be made on a controller?

A. One per verification type

B. As many as needed

C. The same number as firewall policies

D. One less than the number of firewall policies

E. The same number as SSIDs

QUESTION 43

Which of the given cannot be accomplished from the startup wizard?

A. Basic controller configuration

B. License installation

C. VPN configuration

D. WLAN configuration

E. Firewall Roles

QUESTION 44

Users connecting to a remote AP at a branch office can get an IP address through which of the given procedures? (Pick three)

A. DHCP server connected to the Remote AP's controller

B. DHCP server at a branch office

C. Address needs to be statically allotted

D. DHCP server inside the Remote AP

E. DHCP from global content server for Remote Aps

QUESTION 45

Which of the given could be suitable for standalone MAC Verification?

A. Guest User

B. Internal User

C. Barcode scanner

D. Admin user

E. Laptops

QUESTION 46

Which ARM function converts APs with excess capacity into Air Monitors?

A. Airtime fairness

B. Coordinated access to a single channel

C. Co-channel interference mitigation

D. User aware scanning

E. Band Steering

QUESTION 47

What is the purpose of the valid user ACL?

A. When a user transmits data through the controller, the valid user ACL is used to check if the user is in the layer 3 user-table

B. Before a user is added to the controller's user table, the valid user ACL is checked to make sure the user has a valid IP address

C. The valid user ACL is used for the duration of 802.1X verification to check that the user is in the layer 3 user-table

D. When an AP needs to transmit data to a user, it checks the valid user ACL to make sure the user has a valid IP address

E. A list of organized MAC addresses that define the valid users

QUESTION 48

Time range is implemented directly to which one of the given:

A. ROLE

B. Firewall Policy

C. Firewall Rule

D. Profile

E. Interface

QUESTION 49

Which role is allotted prior to launching the captive portal splash screen?

A. Pre-verification role

B. Post-verification role

C. AAA role

D. AAA-CP role

E. CP default role

QUESTION 50

A reboot of the controller is needed in which of the given situations?
(Pick two)

A. Changing controller IP

B. Changing the VLAN of a Virtual AP Profile

C. Creating of a new AP Group

D. Changing of Controller Role

E. Extending a license range

QUESTION 51

What are some greatest practices when configuring the Aruba Firewall
(Pick two)?:

A. Use aliases when likely

B. Write rules from least specific to most specific

C. Take actions like blacklisting when users violate policies

D. Make a dissimilar policy for each unique rule

E. Make dissimilar policies for access to dissimilar servers

QUESTION 52

Which roles needs to be organized via the startup wizard when captive portal is being organized (Pick Two)

A. Roles are not used on the Aruba system

B. Pre-Verification role

C. Validated role

D. Invalidated role

E. The Logon Role

QUESTION 53

Which is the strongest encryption type?

A. AES

B. TKIP

C. WEP

D. MSCHAPv2

E. DES

QUESTION 54

When could you use the Reject action in a firewall policy?

A. To let hackers know which ports are open on your firewall

B. To let your users know they are in violation of corporate policies

C. To tell downstream routers to use a more suitable router

D. To aid in troubleshooting firewall policy configuration

E. To let the system count the violations

QUESTION 55

Which of the given can be organized in the GUI setup wizard? (Pick three)

A. Timezone

B. WLAN

C. VLAN

D. Loopback address

E. DHCP Option 43

QUESTION 56

Which of the given deployment kinds is NOT a valid option when using the AP Wizard?

A. LAN

B. Remote

C. Roaming

D. Remote Mesh

E. LAN Mesh

QUESTION 57

When configuring roles under 'Access Control' in the Controller's Configuration page, what does the 'show reference' action tell us?

A. Which firewall hits were detected that refer to the role

B. Which profiles refer to the role

C. What policies are inside the role

D. What users are now allotted that role

E. What verification procedures use Roles with these policies

QUESTION 58

Which of these are supported by the Aruba Controller? (Pick two)

A. SNMP

B. HSRP

C. AES Encryption

D. Blowfish encryption

E. BGP

QUESTION 59

When looking at users in the 'Monitoring Users' section of the Controller, which of the given information is NOT visible?

A. Role

B. MAC address

C. Output power of user radio

D. Method of verification

E. Age

QUESTION 60

What Controller modes of operation are accessible from the startup wizard (Pick three)?

A. Primary

B. Standalone

C. Master

D. Local

E. Backup controller

ANSWERS

1. Correct Answer: CD
2. Correct Answer: A
3. Correct Answer: C
4. Correct Answer: D
5. Correct Answer: B
6. Correct Answer: E
7. Correct Answer: AD
8. Correct Answer: BD
9. Correct Answer: B
10. Correct Answer: BC
11. Correct Answer: B
12. Correct Answer: C
13. Correct Answer: C
14. Correct Answer: C
15. Correct Answer: ABC
16. Correct Answer: D
17. Correct Answer: AC
18. Correct Answer: BC
19. Correct Answer: BC
20. Correct Answer: AC
21. Correct Answer: D
22. Correct Answer: B
23. Correct Answer: D
24. Correct Answer: B
25. Correct Answer: D
26. Correct Answer: B
27. Correct Answer: A
28. Correct Answer: A
29. Correct Answer: B
30. Correct Answer: ACD
31. Correct Answer: ABD
32. Correct Answer: E
33. Correct Answer: ACDE
34. Correct Answer: D
35. Correct Answer: E
36. Correct Answer: B
37. Correct Answer: A
38. Correct Answer: B
39. Correct Answer: ABD

40. Correct Answer: C
41. Correct Answer: B
42. Correct Answer: B
43. Correct Answer: C
44. Correct Answer: ABD
45. Correct Answer: C
46. Correct Answer: C
47. Correct Answer: B
48. Correct Answer: C
49. Correct Answer: A
50. Correct Answer: AD
51. Correct Answer: AC
52. Correct Answer: BC
53. Correct Answer: A
54. Correct Answer: D
55. Correct Answer: ABC
56. Correct Answer: C
57. Correct Answer: B
58. Correct Answer: AC
59. Correct Answer: C
60. Correct Answer: BCD